# Christmas Book

## 9 Jazzy Piano Solos with Optional CD Accompaniments

## Arranged by Mike Springer

Jazz music is fun to play year round, especially at Christmas time. From driving swing to jazz waltz, the *Not Just Another Christmas Book* series has it all. The carefully crafted arrangements are perfect for Christmas parties and recitals, or they can be used simply for fun.

Additionally, the books are truly unique because they contain accompanying CDs that feature bass and drum parts to create the sense of playing in a jazz trio. Each tune has three different CD tracks in the following order:

- For listening, the *Performance Model* track features the piano, bass, and drums in a complete performance.
- For practicing, a *Practice Tempo* track features the bass and drums (without the piano part) at a slow tempo.
- For performing, the *Performance Tempo* track features the bass and drums (without the piano part).

For practice and performance ease, a two-measure drum lead-in is given at the beginning of every CD track. Metronome marks for both tempos are given at the beginning of each arrangement.

# Contents

For my mentor and friend, Dr. Jerry Wallace

Produced by
Alfred Music Publishing Co., Inc.
P.O. Box 10003
Van Nuys, CA 91410-0003
alfred.com

Printed in USA.

ISBN-10: 0-7390-8114-4
ISBN-13: 978-0-7390-8114-3

Cover photos
scizzors cutting paper: © istockphoto.com / hatman12 • ribbon: © istockphoto.com / egal • Christmas wrapping: © istockphoto.com / fotoAta

# Jolly Old St. Nicholas

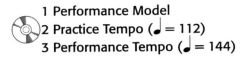

1 Performance Model
2 Practice Tempo (♩ = 112)
3 Performance Tempo (♩ = 144)

Traditional
Arr. Mike Springer

# Away in a Manger

4 Performance Model
5 Practice Tempo (♩ = 76)
6 Performance Tempo (♩ = 100)

**Traditional**
Arr. Mike Springer

5

# Joy to the World

7 Performance Model
8 Practice Tempo ( ♩ = 120)
9 Performance Tempo ( ♩ = 160)

Music by G. F. Handel
Arr. Mike Springer

# Deck the Hall

10 Performance Model
11 Practice Tempo (♩ = 104)
12 Performance Tempo (♩ = 132)

Traditional Old Welsh Carol
Arr. Mike Springer

# Up on the Housetop

13 Performance Model
14 Practice Tempo (♩ = 120)
15 Performance Tempo (♩ = 176)

Words and Music by Benjamin R. Hanby
Arr. Mike Springer

# Ukrainian Bell Carol

16 Performance Model
17 Practice Tempo ($\quarternote = 100$)
18 Performance Tempo ($\quarternote = 120$)

**Traditional**
Arr. Mike Springer

# Jingle Bell Rock

19 Performance Model
20 Practice Tempo (♩ = 112)
21 Performance Tempo (♩ = 144)

Words and Music by
Joe Beal and Jim Boothe
Arr. Mike Springer

# Frosty the Snowman

22 Performance Model
23 Practice Tempo (♩ = 112)
24 Performance Tempo (♩ = 152)

Words and Music by
Steve Nelson and Jack Rollins
Arr. Mike Springer

# What Child Is This?

25 Performance Model
26 Practice Tempo (♩ = 100)
27 Performance Tempo (♩ = 120)

Traditional
Arr. Mike Springer

21